The St. Martin's Pocket Guide to

Library Research
and

Documenting Sources

Prepared by Virginia Biggar

Manufactured in the United States of America.

5   4   3   2   1

f   e   d   c   b

For information, write to:

St. Martin's Press, Inc.
175 Fifth Avenue
New York, NY 10010

ISBN: 0–312–05688–5

Contents

7. Note-and-Bibliography Style — 70

1. Library Reference Sources

Consulting reference books is a useful first step in constructing a working bibliography for your research paper. This section is a guide to the reference sources available in most libraries. The sources listed all provide bibliographies by discipline that will help you to identify books and articles that apply to your topic.

In addition to consulting the volumes listed in this section for potential sources, ask your instructor and a reference librarian for advice. Often they will be able to lead you quickly to the most relevant and specific reference book for your topic.

1.1. General guides to reference books and indexes

These guides list reference sources by discipline.

Bibliographic Index: A Cumulative Bibliography of Bibliographies

The New York Times Guide to Reference Material

Sheehy, Eugene P., ed. *Guide to Reference Books*. 10th ed. 1986.

Walford's Guide to Reference Material. 4th ed. 1980–1987.

For example, the *Bibliographic Index's* section on history includes the *Harvard Guide to American History* as one of its entries. The *Harvard Guide* provides bibliographies for subjects in American history, such as the Vietnam War; under that heading you would find a list of articles on that subject.

1.2. General encyclopedias

The following sources provide general information on alphabetically arranged subjects.

Collier's Encyclopedia
Encyclopedia Britannica
Encyclopedia Americana

1.3. Disciplinary encyclopedias

These specialized volumes contain more specific entries and more complete bibliographies than general encyclopedias.

Dictionary of American History
Encyclopedia of American Art
Encyclopedia of Anthropology
Encyclopedia of Banking and Finance
Encyclopedia of Bioethics
Encyclopedia of the Biological Sciences
Encyclopedia of Chemistry
Encyclopedia of Computer Science and Technology
Encyclopedia of Crime and Justice
Encyclopedia of Earth Sciences
Encyclopedia of Economics
Encyclopedia of Education
Encyclopedia of Educational Research
Encyclopedia of Geographic Information
Encyclopedia of Management
Encyclopedia of the Middle Ages
Encyclopedia of Philosophy
Encyclopedia of Physical Education, Fitness and Sports

Encyclopedia of Physics
Encyclopedia of Psychology
Encyclopedia of Religion and Ethics
Encyclopedia of Social Work
Encyclopedia of World Art
Harvard Guide to American History
International Encyclopedia of Film
International Encyclopedia of the Social Sciences
McGraw-Hill Encyclopedia of Environmental Science
McGraw-Hill Encyclopedia of Science and Technology
McGraw-Hill Encyclopedia of World Drama
New Grove Dictionary of Music and Musicians
New Illustrated Encyclopedia of World History

1.4. General periodical indexes

Periodical indexes are guides to journal, newspaper, and magazine articles. After identifying articles that seem promising, consult your library's list of periodicals in its collection to see if the publications you want are available. Some indexes and the periodicals they list may be on microfilm or microfiche in your library.

Alternative Press Index
Book Review Digest
Business Index
Humanities Index
The Christian Science Monitor Index
Magazine Index
NewsBank (a monthly index on microfiche of newspapers from over 450 U.S. cities)

Newspaper Index (a monthly index of the *New York Times,* the *Wall Street Journal,* the *Los Angeles Times,* the *Washington Post,* and the *Christian Science Monitor*)

The New York Times Index

The Times Index (London)

Readers' Guide to Periodical Literature

Social Sciences Index

Verticle File Index: A Subject and Title Index to Selected Pamphlet Material

The Wall Street Journal Index

1.5. Specialized periodical indexes and abstracts

Each of the following volumes addresses a specific discipline or subject. Indexes contain bibliographies, whereas abstracts provide bibliographies as well as summaries of each article.

America: History and Life

Applied Science and Technology Index

Art Index

Biological Abstracts

Biological and Agricultural Index

Business Periodicals Index

Chemical Abstracts

Communications Abstracts

Computer Literature Index

Cumulative Index to Nursing and Allied Health Literature

Current Index to Journals in Education

Dissertation Abstracts International

Ecology Abstracts
Education Index
Engineering Index Monthly and Author Index
Essay and General Literature Index
General Science Index
Historical Abstracts
Index Medicus
Index to Child Welfare
Index to Governmental Periodicals
Index to Legal Periodicals
International Bibliography of Economics
McGill's Bibliography of Literary Criticism
MLA International Bibliography
Music Index
Philosopher's Index
Physical Education Index
Physics Abstracts
Pollution Abstracts
Political Science—A Bibliographic Guide to the Literature
Psychological Abstracts
Public Affairs Information Service (PAIS)
Religious and Theological Abstracts
Science Abstracts
Sociological Abstracts

1.6. Biographical indexes and dictionaries

Biography Index, 1946–date
A Cumulative Index to Biographical Material in Books and Magazines
Current Biography, 1940–date

Dictionary of American Biography, 1928–1937 plus supplements

Dictionary of National Biography (for Great Britain), 1882–1900 plus supplements

International Who's Who, 1935–date

Webster's Biographical Dictionary

Who's Who (for Great Britain), 1849–date

Who's Who in America, 1899–date

1.7. Statistical information guides

Editorial Research Reports

Facts on File Yearbook

Statesman's Year-Book

Statistical Abstract of the United States

World Almanac and Book of Facts

1.8. Databases

Many libraries have access to databases through an online search. These databases are indexes of material that can be searched for key words, titles, and authors that relate to your topic. The advantage of searching for source material on a database is the abundance of information the database can store, and therefore the completeness of the list of sources it will provide. The disadvantage is the often high cost of conducting a search. Ask your reference librarian about the cost and practicality of a database search. Here are two common database services.

Educational Resources Information Center (ERIC)

National Technical Information Service (NTIS)

1.9. Card catalogs

Card catalogs list a library's available materials in three ways: by author, by title, and by subject. In addition to publication information, each card lists a call number in the upper left-hand corner that indicates where the book is kept in the library stacks. The cards will either be filed together, or author and title cards will be filed together and subject cards separately.

Many libraries have a computerized catalog as well as a card catalog. Because many libraries are still in the process of computerizing, ask your librarian to tell you what is listed in the computerized catalog and what is in the card catalog.

2. Plagiarism and Incorporating Source Material

2.1. Plagiarism

Plagiarism is the use of another person's words or ideas without crediting your source, thereby representing the words and ideas as your own. Avoid plagiarism in your research paper by keeping careful track of the material you gather from sources as you take notes for, write, and edit your paper.

2.2. Incorporating source material

Information that must be credited to the original source includes another person's exact words, facts that are not widely known or that are the subject of debate; another person's claims or opinions; statistics, figures, or tables from any source.

Information from sources can be incorporated into your paper in three forms: direct quotation, paraphrase, or summary. When you quote someone directly, use the exact wording, spelling, and punctuation used in the source. To avoid confusion when you begin drafting, put quotation marks around any quotation you note down during your research. A paraphrase is a restatement in your own words of an author's ideas as expressed in a specific passage. A summary conveys in your own words a short version of the general ideas from a longer selection. Each of these forms requires a parenthetical or numerical citation in the text to acknowledge the source.

2.2.a. Direct quotation

Integrate short quotations directly into your text, making sure you enclose them in quotation marks. Place the citation after the quotation but before the period ending the sentence.

```
Knightley notes that the media turned its

attention to Vietnam after "the revolt of

the army paratroopers in Saigon in November

1960" (374).
```

Type quotations of more that four lines (in MLA style) or of more than forty words (in APA style) in a block set off from your text. Do not use quotation marks. (See sections 5.1.b and 6.1.b for style guidelines). The following passage conforms to MLA style. The parenthetical reference is typed two spaces after the final punctuation mark.

```
According to Knightley:

          It was only after the revolt of

          army paratroopers in Saigon in

          November 1960, when some 400

          civilians were killed before the

          rebels were overcome, that the

          American press showed the first

          signs of interest in what was

          really going on in Vietnam. The

          New York Times sent out a veteran
```

war correspondent, Homer Bigart,
formerly with the Herald Tribune,
who joined a tiny corps of full-
time reporters in Saigon.

(Knightley 374)

2.2.b. Paraphrase

Here is a paraphrase of the direct quotation cited above.

The New York Times was the first American
daily newspaper to send a full-time correspondent to Vietnam. This move by the
Times was partly in response to a military
incident in November 1960 in which four
hundred civilians were killed. Up until
then, the American press relied on only a
handful of full-time reporters to report on
possible military escalation in Vietnam
(Knightley 374).

2.2.c. Summary

Here is a summary of the longer section from which the
direct quotation above was taken.

Correspondents working in Vietnam during
the earliest years of American involvement

in the 1960s were constantly at odds with the American mission in Saigon and the White House. While they reported that U.S. involvement was escalating, and that Diem was a corrupt president, and questioned the effectiveness of U.S. involvement, the official line from the White House stated the opposite. The Saigon mission impeded access to information and accused these reporters of being unpatriotic and on the wrong side (Knightley 375-382).

3. Overview of Documentation Styles

The following documentation styles for research papers all call for in-text citations and corresponding entries in a final list of bibliographic entries or notes.

As a researcher in any discipline, your documentation goals are twofold: to credit every source you refer to in your paper to avoid plagiarism, and to provide enough information so that your reader can locate these sources. Different disciplines, however, require different styles of source documentation. If you are unsure about which of the following sets of guidelines you should use, check with your instructor.

3.1. Modern Language Association (MLA)

The MLA advocates a system of parenthetical citations of author and page number in the text, with a complete alphabetical list of Works Cited at the end of the paper. Favored in most disciplines in the humanities, especially languages and literature. Humanities also include philosophy, religion, and history. Complete guidelines are in the *MLA Handbook for Writers of Research Papers*, 3rd ed. (New York: MLA, 1988).

3.2. American Psychological Association (APA)

The APA adheres to a system of parenthetical citations of author and year of publication in the text, with a complete alphabetical list of References at the end of the paper. Favored in most social sciences, especially psychology. Social sciences also include sociology, political science, and economics. Complete guidelines are in the *Publication Manual of the American Psychological Association*, 3rd ed. (Washington, DC: APA, 1983).

3.3. Note-and-Bibliography

Also known as Old MLA style because the MLA required this style until 1984, the note-and-bibliography style consists of references in the text numbered consecutively with superscript (raised) numbers. Each citation corresponds to a numbered entry in a list of Notes at the end of the paper. A Bibliography (an alphabetical list of works cited) may be included as well. Used for history research papers and in some other humanities. See the *MLA Handbook for Writers of Research Papers*, 3rd ed. (New York: MLA, 1988) for complete guidelines.

3.4. Council of Biology Editors (CBE)

The CBE outlines a standard documentation style and some common variations found in many natural- and applied-science journals. The number system consists of in-text citations of numbers that correspond to a numbered Literature Cited list either arranged sequentially—according to the order in which the works are first cited in the text—or arranged alphabetically by author and then assigned numbers. The name-and-year system (also known as the Harvard System), consists of in-text citations of author and year of publication that correspond to a Literature Cited list arranged alphabetically by author. Check with your instructor about which style to use. Complete guidelines can be found in the *CBE Style Manual: A Guide for Authors, Editors, and*

Publishers in the Biological Sciences, 5th ed., rev. and exp. (Bethesda, MD: CBE, 1983).

For chemistry or physics papers consult the following:

American Chemical Society. *Handbook for Authors*. Washington, DC: ACS, 1978.

American Institute of Physics. *Style Manual*. New York: AIP, 1978.

4. Abbreviations

This section lists abbreviations commonly used in scholarly works. MLA, APA, note-and-bibliography, and CBE styles all have different guidelines for abbreviation use in bibliographic entries. Follow carefully the guidelines of the particular style you are using.

4.1. Time

AD	*anno Domini* ("in the year of the Lord") (used before date: AD 1176)
a.m.	*ante meridiem* ("before noon")
BC	before Christ (used after date: 210 BC)
BCE	before Common Era
CE	Common Era
p.m.	*post meridiem* ("after noon")

4.2. Scholarly and reference terms

b.	born
BA	Bachelor of Arts
bib.	biblical
BS	Bachelor of Science
C	Centigrade
c., ca.	*circa* ("about"); used with dates
d.	died
diss.	dissertation
e.g.	*exempli gratia* ("for example")
et al.	*et alii/et aliae* ("and others")
etc.	*et cetera* ("and so forth")
F	Fahrenheit
HR	House of Representatives

H. Rept.	House Report
H. Res.	House Resolution
i.e.	*id est* ("that is")
JD	*Juris Doctor* ("Doctor of Law")
Jr.	Junior
LC	Library of Congress
MA	Master of Arts
MD	*Medicinae Doctor* ("Doctor of Medicine")
MS	Master of Science
ms., mss.	manuscript(s)
NB	*nota bene* ("take notice")
n.d.	no date of publication
PS	postscript
qtd.	quoted
S. Doc.	Senate Document
Sr.	Senior
S. Rept.	Senate Report
S. Res.	Senate Resolution
vs. (v.)	versus

4.3. Acronyms and initial abbreviations

If a term, a title, or the name of an organization can be shortened to an acronym or initial abbreviation, it is appropriate to do so after the first reference in your paper. If you use a term only once or twice, spell it out each time. Otherwise, spell the name out once in full, providing the abbreviation you will use from then on in parentheses following the term. For example:

```
Nixon and Kissinger negotiated the

Strategic Arms Limitation Talks (SALT) in

1972.
```

4.4. Geographical names

Always spell out geographical names in your text, with the exception of USSR, and in papers discussing the period 1949–1990, BRD (West Germany) and DDR (East Germany). Use these abbreviations in bibliographic entries requiring state or country identification.

Afr.	Africa
AK	Alaska
AL	Alabama
AR	Arkansas
Aus.	Austria
Austral.	Australia
AZ	Arizona
Belg.	Belgium
BRD	Bundesrepublik Deutschland (also W. Ger.) (1949–1990)
Bulg.	Bulgaria
CA	California
Can.	Canada
CO	Colorado
CT	Connecticut
Czech.	Czechoslovakia
DDR	Deutsche Demokratische Republik (also E. Ger.) (1949–1990)
DE	Delaware
DC	District of Columbia
E. Ger.	East Germany (also DDR) (1949–1990)
Eng.	England
FL	Florida
Fr.	France
GA	Georgia
Gt. Brit.	Great Britain
HI	Hawaii

Hung.	Hungary
IA	Iowa
ID	Idaho
IL	Illinois
IN	Indiana
Ire.	Ireland
Isr.	Israel
It.	Italy
Jap.	Japan
KS	Kansas
KY	Kentucky
LA	Louisiana
MA	Massachusetts
MD	Maryland
ME	Maine
Mex.	Mexico
MI	Michigan
MN	Minnesota
MO	Missouri
MS	Mississippi
MT	Montana
NC	North Carolina
ND	North Dakota
NE	Nebraska
NH	New Hampshire
NJ	New Jersey
NM	New Mexico
NV	Nevada
NY	New York
OH	Ohio
OK	Oklahoma
OR	Oregon
PA	Pennsylvania
Pol.	Poland

PRC	People's Republic of China
RI	Rhode Island
SC	South Carolina
SD	South Dakota
TN	Tennessee
TX	Texas
UK	United Kingdom
US	United States
USSR	Union of Soviet Socialist Republics
UT	Utah
VA	Virginia
VT	Vermont
WA	Washington
W. Ger.	West Germany (also BRD) (1949–1990)
WI	Wisconsin
WV	West Virginia
WY	Wyoming
Yug.	Yugoslavia

5. Modern Language Association (MLA) Style

5.1. Documentation

5.1.a. Works Cited

The following are guidelines based on the *MLA Handbook for Writers of Research Papers*, 3rd ed. (New York: MLA, 1988) for citing various types of publications in your alphabetical list of Works Cited.

Books

MLA citations for books require three essential elements: author, title, and publication information (city, publisher, publication date). List the author's surname first, followed by a comma and the author's first name or initials. Then list the title and any subtitle, underlining it if the source is a book, play, or long poem, or enclosing it in quotation marks if it is a short story, poem, or work in a collection. Capitalize all major words.

List the city given on the title page (or the first city if more than one are listed), and include the state or country if the city is an unfamiliar one. Shorten the publisher's name by dropping any initial article and words such as *Press, Publisher, Inc., Company* (but use *UP* for *University Press*), and by using the first or only surname if the company is named for a person or persons (*Norton* for *W. W. Norton; Farrar* for *Farrar, Straus & Giroux*).

Start each entry flush with the left margin and indent each subsequent line five spaces. End each element with a period. Two spaces follow a period when it ends an element; one space follows commas, colons, and semicolons.

— Book by one author

```
Redmon, Coates.  Come as You Are: The Peace

     Corps Story.  San Diego: Harcourt,

     1986.
```

— Two or more books by the same author

Give the author's name in the first entry, and substitute three hyphens followed by a period in entries thereafter. If the role of the author changes from, for example, author to editor, substitute three hyphens, add a comma, and give the notation for editor (*ed.*). Arrange the entries alphabetically by title.

```
Fitzgerald, F. Scott.  The Last Tycoon.

     New York: Scribner's, 1941.

---.  This Side of Paradise.  New York:

     Scribner's, 1920.
```

If a single author of a work listed is also a coauthor of the next work in your list, repeat that author's full name in the new entry. Similarly, if you also cite a work by the author as part of a different group, use his or her full name in each entry. Use three hyphens only when the authors are exactly the same as in the preceding entry.

— Book by two or three authors

Reverse the first author's name, but list the others in regular order. Separate the names with commas.

Begon, Michael, John L. Harper, and Colin
    R. Townsend. _Ecology: Individuals,
    Populations, and Communities_. Sunder-
    land, MA: Sinauer, 1986.

— Book by four or more authors

Give the first author's name and substitute _et al._ for the
other authors.

Bush, Richard C., et al. _The Religious
    World: Communities of Faith_. 2nd ed.
    New York: Macmillan, 1988.

You may also list the full names of all the authors.

Bush, Richard C., Joseph F. Byrnes, Hyla S.
    Converse, Kenneth Dollarhide, Azim
    Nanji, Robert F. Weir, and Kyle M.
    Yates, Jr. _The Religious World: Com-
    munities of Faith_. 2nd ed. New York:
    Macmillan, 1988.

— Two or more books by the same authors

Wayne, Stephen, and George C. Edwards.
    _Presidential Leadership: Politics and
    Policy Making_. New York: St.
    Martin's, 1985.

```
---.   Studying the Presidency.  New York:

       St. Martin's, 1983.
```

— Book by a group

```
St. Martin's Press.  The St. Martin's Guide

     for Authors of College Textbooks.  New

     York: St. Martin's, 1985.
```

— Book with an unidentified author

```
Hammond Compact Road Atlas and Vacation

     Guide.  Maplewood, NJ: Hammond, 1975.
```

— Book prepared by an editor

```
Wynn, Ellen C., ed.  The Short Story: 50

     Masterpieces.  New York: St. Martin's,

     1983.
```

For a work with both an editor and an author, list the work by the person whose work you are citing. If you cite the author's text, list the author first and add the notation *Ed.* and the editor's name in regular order after the title.

```
James, Henry.  The Portrait of a Lady.  Ed.

     Leon Edel.  Boston: Houghton, 1963.
```

If you refer to the editor's words, list the editor first and add *By* and the author's name after the title.

Edel, Leon, ed. <u>The Portrait of a Lady</u>.

By Henry James. Boston: Houghton,

1963.

— Introduction, preface, foreword, or afterword

First list the author and name of the part cited (neither underlined nor in quotation marks). Add *By* and the book's author after the title. If the book's author and the part's author are the same, give only the last name. List the inclusive page numbers of the part cited.

Branch, Taylor. Preface. <u>Parting the</u>

<u>Waters: America in the King Years,</u>

<u>1954-63</u>. By Branch. New York: Simon,

1988. xi-xii.

— Work in an edited collection

Name the author and the work you are citing first, enclosing the selection title in quotation marks if it is a poem, short story, or essay, or underlining it if it was originally published as a book, such as a play or a novel. Add *Ed.* and the editor's name after the book title. Note the inclusive page numbers of the selection.

Wilson, August. <u>Fences</u>. <u>The Bedford Intro-</u>

<u>duction to Drama</u>. Ed. Lee A. Jacobus.

New York: Bedford-St. Martin's, 1989.

1043-1073.

— Multivolume work

If you use two or more volumes of a multivolume work, include the total number of volumes after the title. If the volumes were published over two or more years, note the inclusive publication dates (1984-86).

```
Roberts, Randy, and James S. Olson, eds.

    American Experiences.  2 vols.  Glen-

    view, IL: Scott, 1986.
```

— One volume of a multivolume work

If you use only one volume of a multivolume work, note the volume number after the title and the total number of volumes at the end of the citation.

```
Roberts, Randy, and James S. Olson, eds.

    American Experiences.  Vol. 2.  Glen-

    view, IL: Scott, 1986.  2 vols.
```

— Edition

```
Peretz, Don.  The Middle East Today.  4th

    ed.  New York: Praeger, 1983.
```

— Translation

If you cite the author's work, list the author first and add *Trans.* and the translator's name after the title.

```
Le Roy Ladurie, Emmanuel.  Montaillou: The

    Promised Land of Error.  Trans. Bar-
```

bara Bray.   New York: Vintage-Random,

1979.

If you refer primarily to the comments or word choice of the translator, list the translator first and include *By* and the author's name after the book title.

Bray, Barbara, trans.   <u>Montaillou: The

Promised Land of Error</u>.   By Emmanuel

Le Roy Ladurie.   New York: Vintage-

Random, 1979.

— Republished book

List the original publication date before the publication information of the book cited.

Walker, Alice.   <u>You Can't Keep a Good Woman

Down</u>.   1971.   San Diego: Harvest-

Harcourt, 1981.

— Book in a series

List the series title, and any series number, after the book title, neither underlining the series title nor enclosing it in quotation marks.

Glassman, Bruce S.   <u>J. Paul Getty: Oil Bil-

lionaire</u>.   The American Dream.

Englewood Cliffs, NJ: Silver, 1989.

— Publisher's imprint

Many publishers publish groups of books under different imprints, or names. Hyphenate the imprint and the publisher.

```
Hersey, John.  Blues.  New York: Borzoi-
     Knopf, 1987.
```

— Item from a reference book

List the item by author, or if the item is unsigned, by title. For well-known reference books, give only the edition, if one is stated, and the year. Give full publication information for less well-known reference books. You need not give page numbers if the work is arranged alphabetically.

```
Callahan, James Morton.  "The West as a Fac-
     tor in American Politics."  Encyclo-
     pedia Americana.  1955 ed.
"Paleontology."  Random House Dictionary of
     the English Language.  1987 ed.
```

— Government publication

List the author first, if given. Otherwise, list the government, agency, title of publication, number and session of Congress if appropriate, type of source (bill, resolution, report, or document), number if there is one, and publication information. The *Congressional Record* requires only the date and page number(s).

```
United States.  Cong.  Senate.  Committee
     on Foreign Relations.  Hearings on Ar-
```

mament and Disarmament Problems. 90th

Cong., 1st sess. Washington: GPO,

1967.

— Pamphlet

Educational Testing Service. Borrowing for

Education. Princeton, NJ: ETS, 1989.

— Unpublished dissertation

Cahn, Anne. "Eggheads and Warheads: Scien-

tists and the ABM." Diss. MIT, 1971.

— Published dissertation

Treat a published dissertation as a book, adding *Diss.*,
the university, and the date before the publication information. If the dissertation was published by UMI
(University Microfilms International), give the order
number at the end of the entry.

Botts, Roderic C. Influences in the Teach-

ing of English, 1917-1935: An Illusion

of Progress. Diss. Northeastern U,

1970. Ann Arbor: UMI, 1971. 71-1799.

— Published proceedings of conference

Spelman, Elizabeth V. "Plato and Aristotle

on Women." Abstract. Proceedings and

<u>Addresses of the American Philosophi-</u>

<u>cal Association</u>. Vol. 63. No. 2.

Newark, DE: APA, 1989. 57-58.

— Book published before 1900

Omit the publisher's name and use a comma after the
city of publication.

Eliot, George. <u>Middlemarch</u>. London, 1871-

72.

— Non-English book

Follow the style of capitalization of the original work,
and add the English title in brackets after the title, if
needed for clarification.

Kafka, Franz. <u>Das Schloss</u> [The Castle].

Frankfurt am Main: Fischer, 1982.

Periodicals

MLA citations for periodicals require three essential
elements: author, title, and publication information,
which includes inclusive page numbers. List the
author's surname first, followed by a comma, the
author's first name (or initials), and a period. Then list
the title and any subtitle of the article in quotation
marks. Capitalize all major words. End with a period.

The journal title, volume number, publication date,
and page numbers comprise the publication information. List the journal title as it appears in the periodical,
omitting any initial *A*, *An*, or *The*, and capitalize all
major words. Underline the title. Skip one space and

give the volume number, followed by a space, the date in parentheses, a colon, a space, and the inclusive page numbers. Do not use *p.* or *pp.*

Start each entry flush with the left margin and indent subsequent lines five spaces. End the entry with a period. Two spaces follow a period when it ends an element; one space follows commas, colons, and semicolons.

— Article in a journal with continuous pagination

```
Gatewood, Willard B., Jr.  "Aristocrats of
     Color: South and North: The Black
     Elite, 1880-1920."  Journal of
     Southern History 54 (1988): 3-20.
```

— Article in a journal paginated by issue

For journals that number each issue separately, follow the volume number with a period and the issue number.

```
Stevenson, Adlai E., and Alton Frye.  "Trad-
     ing with the Communists."  Foreign Af-
     fairs 68.2 (1989): 53-71.
```

— Article from a newspaper

List the title of a newspaper as it is stated on the front page, omitting any initial *A*, *An*, or *The*, and underline it. If the city of publication of a locally published newspaper is not included in the title, add it in brackets after the title. Give the complete date (day, abbreviated month, year). If the front page lists an edition (late ed., national ed.), add a comma and the edition notation after the date. Give the inclusive page numbers, or the first page number and a plus sign if the article runs on discontinuous pages.

```
Hemingway, Sam.  "Slain British 'Spy'

    Trailed."  Burlington Free Press 15

    Apr. 1990: A1+.
```

— Article from a magazine

Use the following format for a weekly or biweekly magazine.

```
Begley, Adam.  "Black Studies' New Star."

    New York Times Magazine 1 Apr. 1990:

    24+.
```

For a magazine published monthly or bimonthly, give only the month and the year.

— Article from a magazine, unidentified author

```
"Gorbachev's Greatest Gamble."  Economist

    24-30 Mar. 1990: 14-17.
```

— Editorial or letter to the editor

Add the designation *Editorial* or *Letter* after the title, if there is one, or in place of a missing title.

```
"Mitterand's East Bank."  Editorial.  Wall

    Street Journal 6 Apr. 1990, eastern

    ed.: A18.
```

Hildebrand, David. Letter. <u>Pennsylvania</u>
   <u>Gazette</u>. Feb.-Mar. 1990: 17.

— Review

Robinson, Marilynne. "The Guilt She Left
   Behind." Rev. of <u>Because It Is Bit-</u>
   <u>ter, and Because It Is My Heart</u>, by
   Joyce Carol Oates. <u>New York Times</u>
   <u>Book Review</u> 23 Apr. 1990: 7-9.

If the review is unsigned and untitled, begin the entry
with *Rev of.*

Other sources

The following sources do not fall under the book or
periodical categories. Follow the guidelines particular
to each entry.

— Computer software

Sargent, Steven D. <u>The First Crusade: The</u>
   <u>Great Expedition to Jerusalem</u>. Vers.
   1.0. Computer software. Clearinghouse for Academic Software, 1987.
   Digital VAX.

— Material from a computer service

List the source as you would printed material, adding the service's identification number.

"Thomas Jefferson." _Academic American En-_

cyclopedia. 1981. CompuServe record

no. 1823.

— Material from an information service

For previously published material, list the work's publication information and add the service's reference number. For unpublished material, list the information service and date before the reference number.

Belenky, Mary F. "The Role of Deafness in

the Moral Development of Hearing Im-

paired Children and Adolescents."

Teaching, Learning and Development.

Ed. A. Areson and J. DeCaro.

Rochester, NY: National Institute for

the Deaf, 1984. ERIC ED 248 646.

— Material from NewsBank

Treat the article as you would one from a newspaper, adding the _Newsbank_ name, form description, heading, and article location.

Sharpe, Lora. "A Quilter's Tribute." _Bos-_

ton Globe 25 Mar. 1989. NewsBank

```
[Microform], Social Relations, 1989,
fiche 6, grids B4-6.
```

— Letter

Treat a published letter as a work in a collection, but add the date of the letter after the title.

```
Kennan, George.   "Letter to his sister."
     7 Dec. 1940.   Sketches from a Life.
     New York: Pantheon, 1989.   47-53.
```

Treat a letter written to yourself as follows:

```
Leakey, Richard.   Letter to the author.   24
     July 1985.
```

For a letter from an archival collection, identify the letter, give the date, then list the name of the collection and the name and city of the institution that houses the collection.

```
Higginson, Henry Lee.   Letter to his
     father.   29 Sept. 1889.   Henry Lee Hig-
     ginson Papers.   Lamont Library,
     Cambridge, MA.
```

— Interview

Treat a published interview as a work in a collection. If the interview is untitled, use the label *Interview*.

```
Tuchman, Barbara.   Interview.   A World of

     Ideas.   By Bill Moyers.   New York:

     Doubleday, 1989.   3-13.
```

Identify a personally conducted interview as such and give the date of the interview.

```
Lehrer, Jim.   Personal interview.   2 Oct.

     1986.
```

Use the following form for a broadcast interview.

```
Lynch, David.   Interview.   All Things Con-

     sidered.   Natl. Public Radio.   WNYC,

     New York.   12 Apr. 1990.
```

— Television or radio program

Use quotation marks for episodes and underline programs.

```
"Comfortable Lies and Bitter Truths."

     Writ. and narr. Hedrick Smith.   Prod.

     and dir. Sherry Jones.   Inside

     Gorbachev's USSR.   Exec. prod. WGBH.

     PBS. WNET, New York.   7 May 1990.
```

— Film, videotape

<u>Driving Miss Daisy</u>. Dir. Bruce Beresford.

    With Jessica Tandy, Morgan Freeman,

    and Dan Aykroyd. Warner, 1989.

To sight an individual's performance, name the individual first.

Freeman, Morgan, actor. <u>Driving Miss

    Daisy</u>. Dir. Bruce Beresford. With

    Jessica Tandy and Dan Aykroyd.

    Warner, 1989

If you cite a videotape or slide program, note the medium, neither underlined nor in quotation marks, after the title.

— Performance

<u>Lettice and Lovage</u>. By Peter Shaffer.

    Dir. Michael Blakemore. With Maggie

    Smith. Barrymore Theater, New York.

    2 Apr. 1990.

To sight an individual's performance, name the individual first.

Blakemore, Michael, dir. <u>Lettice and

    Lovage</u>. By Peter Shaffer. With Maggie Smith. Barrymore Theater, New

York. 2 Apr. 1990.

— Recording

Begin with the person's name whose work is your focus. Use quotation marks for a specific part of a recording. Add *Rec.* and the date of the recording, if known, after the title. Underline record titles, but do not underline or use quotation marks for musical compositions. If the recording is an audiotape or compact disc, note the medium, neither underlined nor in quotation marks, after the title. Provide the manufacturer's name, catalog number, and the year of issue.

Parker, Charlie, alto saxophone. "Blues

for Alice." Rec. Aug. 1951. The

Original Recordings of Charlie Parker.

Polygram, 837176-2, 1988.

Haydn, Franz Joseph. Symphony no. 93 in D

major and Surprise, Symphony no. 94 in

G major. Cond. George Szell.

Cleveland Orch. Columbia, MS 7006.

— Musical composition

Underline any title assigned to a musical composition, but do not underline or enclose in quotation marks works known by form, number, and key.

Haydn, Franz Joseph. <u>Surprise</u>, Symphony

    no. 94 in G Major.

— Work of art

Underline the title of a painting, sculpture, or photograph. List the name of the institution that holds the work, add a comma, and give the city in which the institution is located.

Seurat, Georges. <u>A Sunday Afternoon on the</u>

    <u>Island of La Grande Jatte</u>. Art In-

    stitute of Chicago, Chicago.

— Photograph of a work of art

List the location of the artistic work and give the publication date for the source of the photograph.

Whistler, James A. McNeill. <u>Peacock Room</u>

    <u>from Home of F. R. Leyland</u>. Freer Gal-

    lery of Art, Washington, DC. Illus.

    21-91 in <u>Art through the Ages</u>. 8th

    ed. By Horst de la Croix and Richard

    G. Tansey. San Diego: Harcourt, 1986.

— Lecture, speech, or address

List the speaker, the title in quotation marks if there is one, the name of the institution or group, the place, and the date. If there is no title, use the labels *Lecture, Opening Address,* or other appropriate wording.

Safire, William.   Commence. Address.

    Syracuse Univ.   Syracuse, NY, 6 May

    1990.

5.1.b. Parenthetical citations

A parenthetical citation follows any quotation, paraphrase, summary, or other reference to another's work. Your goal is to give the author credit and the reader enough information to find the complete reference in the list of Works Cited and to locate the exact material in the source itself.

Each citation includes the author (or a short form of the title if no author is given) and a page number. Place the parenthetical citation at the end of a sentence or at a logical break. Punctuation follows the citation's closing parenthesis in running text, but precedes the citation's opening parenthesis in block quotations.

Two ways of incorporating citations are shown in the first two examples that follow. The first shows the author and page number noted in parentheses. Use the second method if you wish to bring more attention to the author by using his or her name in the text. You then need put only the page number in parentheses.

— Author named in citation

Virginia Woolf's radical manifesto on the

history of discrimination experienced by

women writers was a precursor to ideas that

would be championed by later feminists
(Richter 1064).

— Author named in text

Richter asserts that Virginia Woolf's radical manifesto on the history of discrimination experienced by women writers was a
precursor to ideas that would be championed
by later feminists (1064).

— Author of more than one reference
Add a short form of the title after the author's name.

The Red Sox went into the 1967 season "with
a ninth place finish from the previous
season hanging over their heads, and had
little reason to believe that they would
play in the '67 World Series" (Angell, Sum-
mer Game 173).

— Two or three authors

Chayes and Wiesner felt that the decision
to deploy the antiballistic missile system
was based on lack of Soviet compliance with

agreements concerning satellite countries
(29).

— Four or more authors

The administration did not expect to change
the Soviet system but did aim to change the
Soviet Union's concept of international
relations (Brodie et al. 288).

— Unidentified author

More dinosaur remains have been unearthed
in the American Southwest than in any other
part of the world ("Paleontology" 1397).

— Long quotation

If you use a quotation of more than four typed lines in
your paper, type it in block form, indenting each line
ten spaces. Place the parenthetical reference two spaces
after the punctuation at the end of the block. Double-
space the block.

Eudora Welty also feels that the most in-
tense experiences are the result of the con-
vergence of individual experiences:

> Of course the greatest confluence
> of all is that which makes up the

human memory--the individual

human memory. My own is the

treasure most dearly regarded by

me, in my life and in my work as

a writer. Here time, also, is sub-

ject to confluence. The memory is

a living thing--it too is in tran-

sit. But during its moment, all

that is remembered joins, and

lives--the old and the young, the

past and the present.   (Welty 104)

— Literary text

To enable readers to locate parts of a literary work available in different editions, provide the page number of the edition you are using followed by a semicolon and the chapter or section number for a novel (25; ch. 3), and just line numbers for a poem, using the word *line* or *lines* in the first reference (lines 21-22) and numbers alone in subsequent citations. When citing a play, note the title, act, scene, and line numbers.

With the words "the servant that did sting

thy father's life now wears his crown," the

ghost of his father reveals to Hamlet that
his uncle is the murderer of his father
(<u>Hamlet</u> 1.5.40-41).

— Reference to an entire work

In both Louise Erdrich's <u>Tracks</u> and Tony
Hillerman's <u>The Dark Wind</u>, native American
traditions and beliefs are woven into tales
of fiction.

— More than one source in a citation

De Klerk's intention is to share power with
the black majority, not surrender power,
but universal suffrage would mean that at
some point power will change hands in South
Africa (Nelan 149; <u>Freedom Man</u> 15).

— Indirect source for a quotation

Use the abbreviation *qtd. in* ("quoted in") and name the
source.

In a clear expression of cynicism toward
the state of political language, George Or-
well said, "In our time, political speech
and writing are largely the defense of the

indefensible. . . . Thus political language
has to consist largely of euphemism,
question-begging and sheer cloudy vague-
ness" (qtd. in Zinsser 16).

— Source with a volume number

Provide the author's name, the volume number followed by a colon and one space, and the page number.

Langston Hughes's character Jesse B.
Simple, like Huck Finn and George Babbitt,
is an artistic representation of a common
life (Brooks, Lewis, and Warren 2: 2692).

5.1.c. Notes

MLA style permits the use of content and bibliographic
notes to give further explanatory or bibliographic information that adds meaning to the discussion in your text,
but would not fit smoothly in the running text. Keep
your notes brief.

Number notes consecutively in the text with superscript numbers, and list entries consecutively in the list of
Notes, again with superscript numbers. Notes are typed
on a separate page directly before the list of Works Cited.

— Text

Under the usual tight guidance of Henry Kissinger, the Nixon administration came up

with three theories that guided Nixon's
foreign policy.[1]

— Note

Note

[1] For further discussion of the in-
fluence and management style of Henry Kissinger, see Gaddis 275-78.

— Works Cited entry

Work Cited

Gaddis, John L.   <u>Strategies of Containment</u>.
    New York: Oxford UP, 1982.

5.2. Sample Pages

The following instructions apply to the preparation of your entire research paper. Additional instructions for individual sections of the paper are also included in this section.

Margins: One inch on all sides; do not justify lines.

Indentation: Indent the first line of each paragraph five spaces, and each line of a long quotation ten spaces from left margin.

Spacing: Double-space the entire paper, including the heading and title, block quotations, Notes, and Works Cited.

Numbering: Number your pages consecutively, starting on the heading and title page and continuing through the Works Cited list, one-half inch from the top of the page and flush with the right margin. Type your last name, separated by one space, before the page number.

5.2.a. Heading and title

The heading and the title appear at the top of the first page of a research paper; do not use a separate title page.

Heading: Type your name, the instructor's name, the course number, and the date (day, month, year) beginning one inch from the top of the first page and flush with the left margin. Type each item on a separate line; double-space the heading.

Title: Center, a double-space below the date; double-space between lines of the title.

First line of text: Begin one double-space below the title and indent five spaces.

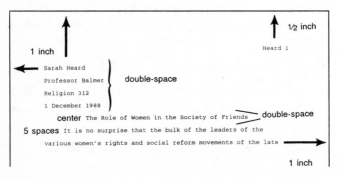

5.2.b. Notes

The list of Notes is typed on a separate page directly before the list of Works Cited.

Title: Center *Notes* (or *Note*, if only one) one inch from the top of the first page only of your list. Double-space to the first note.

Indentation: Indent the first line of each entry five spaces; type subsequent lines within the entry flush with the left margin.

Spacing: Double-space between and within all entries.

Note numbers: Number consecutively, using super-script numbers. Be sure that each number corresponds to the correct note in your text. Add one space between the superscript number and the first word of entry.

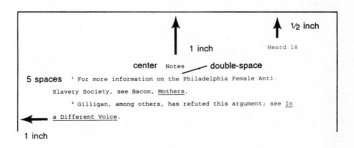

5.2.c. Works Cited

The list of Works Cited begins on a new page after the text and Notes page, if there is one. Arrange it alphabetically by authors' last names or the first word of the title (excluding *A, An, The*), if the author is unknown.

Title: Center *Works Cited* one inch from the top of the first page only of your list. Double-space to the first entry.

Indentation: Begin the first line of each entry flush with the left margin and indent subsequent lines within an entry five spaces.

Spacing: Double-space between and within all entries.

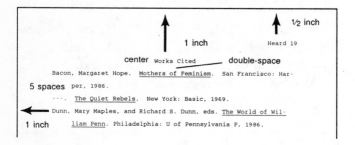

6. American Psychological Association (APA) Style

6.1. Documentation

6.1.a. References

The following are guidelines based on the *Publication Manual of the American Psychological Association*, 3rd ed. (Washington, DC: APA, 1983) for citing various types of publications in your list of References.

Books

APA citations for books require four essential elements: author, date of publication, title, and publication information (city and publisher). List the author's surname first, followed by a comma and first initial(s). Put the publication date in parentheses. Then list the title and any subtitle, underlining it if the source is a book. If it is a work in a collection, do not underline it or enclose it in quotation marks. Capitalize only the first word of the title and subtitle and all proper nouns and proper adjectives.

List the city given on the title page (or the first city if more than one are listed), and include the state or country if the city is an unfamiliar one. Shorten the publisher's name by dropping any initial article and words such as *Publisher, Inc., Company* (*W. W. Norton* for *W. W. Norton & Company, Inc.*). Spell out *Association* and *University Press*.

Start each entry flush with the left margin and indent subsequent lines three spaces. End each element with a period. Two spaces follow a period when it ends an element; one space follows commas, colons, and semicolons.

— Book by one author

Sacks, O. (1978). <u>The man who mistook his
wife for a hat and other clinical tales</u>.
New York: Perennial-Harper & Row.

— Two or more books by the same author

List two or more books by the same author(s) in chronological order.

Galbraith, J. K. (1971). <u>The affluent
society</u>. Boston: Houghton Mifflin.

Galbraith, J. K. (1973). <u>Economics and the
public purpose</u>. Boston: Houghton Mifflin.

— Book by two or more authors

Reverse all authors' names, separate them by commas, and use an ampersand before the last author.

Tullock, G., & McKenzie, R. B. (1985).
<u>The new world of economics</u>. Homewood,
IL: Irwin.

— Book with an unidentified author

<u>Lifesaving: Rescue, training, and water
safety</u>. (1974). New York: American Red
Cross.

— Book by a group

If the corporate author is also the publisher, use the word *Author* after the place of publication.

American Psychiatric Association Task Force
   on Community Services. (1982). <u>A typog-
   raphy of community residential services</u>.
   Washington, DC: Author.

— Book prepared by an editor

Bernheimer, C., & Kahane, C. (Eds.).
   (1985). <u>In Dora's case: Freud-hysteria-
   feminism</u>. New York: Columbia University
   Press.

— Work in an edited collection

Add *pp.* and the selection's inclusive page numbers in parentheses after the book title.

Duquin, M. E. (1989). The importance of
   sport in building women's potential. In
   D. S. Eitzen (Ed.), <u>Sport in contem-
   porary society</u> (pp. 357-362). New York:
   St. Martin's.

— Multivolume work

Add *Vol.* and the inclusive number of volumes in parentheses after the title, before the period that ends the element. If the work was published over a span of years, give the inclusive years (1980-1983).

```
Baltes, P., & Brim, O. G.  (Eds.).  (1980).

    Life-span development and behavior

    (Vols. 1-3).  New York: Academic Press.
```

— One volume of a multivolume work

If the volume has its own title, add a colon and the volume number and title (underlined) after the work's title. If it does not have a title, add *Vol.* and the volume number in parentheses after the work title.

```
Cafagna, A., Peterson, R., & Staudenbauer,

    C. (Eds.).  (1982).  Child nurturance:

    Vol. 1. Philosophy, children, and the

    family.  New York: Plenum Press.
```

— Edition

Place edition information (2nd ed., rev. ed.) in parentheses after the title and one space.

```
Heilbroner, R. L. (1985).  The making of

    economic society (7th ed.).  Englewood

    Cliffs, NJ: Prentice-Hall.
```

— Translation

Place the name of the translator(s) followed by a comma and *Trans.* in parentheses after the title and one space.

Durkheim, E.   (1951).   <u>Suicide</u> (J. A.

   Spaulding & G. Simpson, Trans.).   Glen-

   coe, IL: Free Press of Glencoe.

— Republished book

Note the original publication date in parentheses after
the entry. Do not follow with a period.

Piaget, J.   (1965).   <u>The moral judgment of</u>

   <u>the child</u>.   New York: Free Press.

   (Original work published 1932)

Periodicals

APA citations for periodicals require four essential elements: author, date of publication, title, and publication
information. List the author's surname first, followed by
a comma and first initial(s). Put the publication date in
parentheses. Then list the article's title and any subtitle.
Do not enclose it in quotation marks. Capitalize only the
first word of the title and subtitle, and all proper nouns
and adjectives. End each element with a period.

The journal title, volume number, and inclusive page
numbers comprise the publication information. List the
journal title as it appears in the periodical, omitting any
initial *A*, *An*, or *The*, and capitalize all major words.
Underline the title. Add a comma and a space and give
the volume number (underlined), followed by a
comma, a space, and the inclusive page numbers.

Start each entry flush with the left margin and indent
subsequent lines three spaces. End the entry with a
period. Two spaces follow a period when it ends an
element; one space follows commas, colons, and semi-

colons. For variations on ways of citing volume and issue numbers, dates, and page numbers, see individual entries.

— Article in a journal with continuous pagination

Acker, J. (1988). Class, gender, and the
relations of distribution. Signs, 13,
473-497.

— Article in a journal paginated by issue

If the journal paginates each issue separately, follow the volume number with the issue number in parentheses.

Reece, J. S., & Cool, W. R. (1978).
Measuring investment center performance.
Harvard Business Review, 56(3), 28-40.

— Article from a newspaper

The month and day immediately follow the year of publication. Use the abbreviation *p.* or *pp.* before the page number(s). If the article appears on discontinuous pages, list all pages, separated by commas.

Burns, J. F. (1990, May 6). Afghans seek
direct talks with U.S. on elections.
The New York Times, p. 4.

— Article from a magazine, unidentified author

If an article is unsigned, start with the first word of the title after any initial *A, An,* or *The.* The month (or month and day for a weekly or biweekly magazine) immediately follows the year of publication. Use the abbreviation *pp.* before the inclusive page numbers.

```
Kashmir: Forty years of anger.  (1990,

    March 31-April 6).  Economist, pp. 34-35.
```

— Periodical by a group

```
World Bank.  (1988).  World Development

    Report.  Baltimore: Johns Hopkins Univer-

    sity Press.
```

— English translation of a journal article

```
Kayman, C.  (1984).  After the disaster:

    Arabs in the State of Israel 1948-1950.

    Makhbarot Le-Mekhkar U-Le-Bikoret, 10, 1-

    74.
```

If you use the non-English version of the article, cite that version and give the English translation in brackets after the title.

— Monograph

```
Loevinger, J.  (1962).  Measuring per-

    sonality patterns of women.  Genetic

    Psychology Monographs, 65, 53-136.
```

— Abstract

Baer, H. A. (1989). The American domina-
tive medical system as a reflection of
social relations in the larger society.
Social Science and Medicine, 28(11),
1103-1112. (From Sociological Abstracts,
1990, 38(1), Abstract No. 90V2720)

— Letter to the editor

Enclose an identifying label in brackets after the title,
before the period.

Carter, E. T. (1976). Preventive medicine
[Letter to the editor]. Minnesota
Medicine, 59, 399-401.

Other sources

The following sources do not fall under the book or
periodical categories. Follow the guidelines particular
to each entry.

— Government publication

United States White House Conference on
Aging. (1981). Chartbook on aging in
America: The 1981 Conference on Aging.
Washington, DC: U.S. Government Printing
Office.

If there is a publication number provided, add it in parentheses between the title and the period ending that element.

— Unpublished dissertation

Bullock, B.   (1986).   Basic needs fulfill-
    ment among less developed countries: So-
    cial progress over two decades of
    economic growth.   Unpublished doctoral
    dissertation, Vanderbilt University,
    Nashville.

— Published proceedings of conference

Charles, L. P. (Ed.). (1989).   Proceedings
    of 84th Annual Meeting of American
    Sociological Review.   San Diego, CA:
    Sociological Abstracts.

— Computer software

Hassebrock, F.   (1987).   Human memory and
    experimental psychology [Computer pro-
    gram].   Ames, IA: Clearinghouse for
    Academic Software. (For Digital VAX)

— Material from an information service

Treat material from an information service—such as Educational Resources Information Center (ERIC) or National Technical Information Service (NTIS)—as a printed work, adding the service number in parentheses after the entry. Do not follow with a period.

Belenky, M. F. (1984). The role of deafness in the moral development of hearing
impaired children and adolescents. In
A. Areson & J. DeCaro (Eds.), Teaching,
learning and development (pp. 115-184).
Rochester, NY: National Institute for
the Deaf. (ERIC Document Reproduction
Service No. 248 646)

— Interview

Treat a published interview as a work in a book or periodical, adding a descriptive phrase after the title, if there is one, or in place of the title, if there is none.

Kort, M. (1988, February). Ms. conversa-
tion [Interview with Martina Navratilova
& Billie Jean King]. Ms., pp. 58-62

— Review

Gould, S. J. (1990, April 22). It's not
too late if we're not too crazy [Review

of Making peace with the planet]. The
New York Times Book Review, pp. 15-16.

— Film, videotape

Wells, P., & Weissman, L. (Producers), &
Kasdan, L. (Director). (1990). I love
you to death [Film]. Los Angeles, CA:
Tri-Star Pictures.

— Audiotape, recording

Friedman, M. (1985). Overcoming fear of
success (Tape No. 20284). Brooklyn, NY:
Psychology Today Tapes.

6.1.b. Parenthetical citations

A parenthetical citation follows any quotation, paraphrase,
summary, or other reference to another's work. Your goal
is to give the author credit and the reader enough information to find the complete reference in the list of References
and to locate the exact material in the cited source.

Each citation includes the author (or a short form of
the title if no author is given) and the year of publication, separated by a comma. Two ways of incorporating
citations are shown in the first two examples that follow. The first refers to the author and publication year
in parentheses at the end of the sentence. (The citation
can be placed earlier in the sentence if it fits smoothly
in the text.) Use the second method if you wish to bring

more attention to the author by using his or her name in the text. You need only put the year in parentheses immediately following the author's name.

— Author named in citation

```
Freud viewed psychoanalysis as a fairly one-
sided dialogue (Gay, 1988).
```

If appropriate:
```
It has been suggested (Gay, 1988) that
Freud viewed psychoanalysis as a fairly one-
sided dialogue.
```

— Author named in text

```
Gay (1988) notes that Freud viewed psycho-
analysis as a fairly one-sided dialogue.
```

— Two authors

```
In 1980, a disproportionate share of the
most difficult cities to live in were in
the Northeast and North Central regions of
the country (Nathan & Adams, 1989).
```

— Three to five authors

Note that *and* is spelled out in the text, but an ampersand is used in a citation.

Farkas, Grobe, Sheehan, and Shuan (1990)
report that both noncognitive and cognitive
characteristics determine school success.

For subsequent citations, use only the first author and
et al.

Farkas et al. (1990) report that both noncognitive and cognitive characteristics
determine school success.

— Six or more authors
Cite the first author's name and *et al.* for all citations.

— Corporate author

The World Bank (1988) makes the following
conclusions about sub-Saharan Africa.

— Unidentified author
Use a short form of the title in quotation marks.

A dark picture is painted of the history of
the conflict and its potential to improve
("Kashmir," 1990).

— Reference to a specific page
Include the page number(s) for citations of a particular
part of a source and for all quotations.

In early 1929 a choice had to be made between deliberately engineering a drop in
the stock market or waiting for a un-
avoidable and more serious collapse
(Galbraith, 1988, p. 25).

— Long quotation

If you use a direct quotation of more than forty words
in your paper, type it in block form, indenting each line
of the quotation five spaces from the left margin.
Double-space throughout. Do not use quotation
marks. Place the parenthetical citation two spaces after
the end punctuation of the quotation.

During the 1960s and 1970s,

> Arab primary and secondary educational
> systems expanded rapidly in response
> to larger birth cohorts entering the
> system. This has created job openings
> as teachers and administrators for
> Arab university graduates. In recent
> years, however, the increase in the
> number of public sector jobs in the
> Arab sector has slowed considerably.
> (Shavit, 1990, p. 208)

— More than one source in a citation

List more than one source in the same citation alphabetically by first authors' names. Separate by a semicolon.

At high levels of dependency on foreign capital, development in the Third World has little positive effect on mortality and other aspects of development because elite groups monopolize the fruits of growth (Stokes & Anderson, 1990; Wimberly, 1990).

— Indirect source for a reference

For instance, in 1982 Blau and Blau found that economic inequality is a significant predictor of homicide rates across metropolitan areas (cited in Gartner, 1990).

— Personal communication

Cite as *personal communication* and give the pertinent name and exact date of any material from letters or memos you received or personal or telephone interviews you conducted. You need not list these sources in the References list.

J. L. Morin (personal communication, October 14, 1990) supported with new evidence the claims made in her recent article.

6.1.c. Footnotes

You may use content notes to give information that expands or clarifies part of your text, but would be distracting as part of the running text. Make your notes as brief as possible.

Number notes consecutively in the text with superscript numbers and list entries consecutively in the list of Footnotes, again with superscript numbers. Footnotes are typed on a new page directly after the list of References.

— Text

```
The Strong-Campbell Interest Inventory Test

was administered to twenty women from 23 to

25 years old.¹
```

— Footnote

```
                    Footnote
    ¹Debra Nevas of Teachers College of

Columbia University assisted with ad-

ministering the tests.
```

6.2. Sample pages

The following instructions apply to your whole manuscript. Additional instructions for each individual section of the paper are also included in this section.

Margins: 1½ inches on all sides; do not justify lines. Do not divide words at the end of a line.

Indentation: Indent the first line of each paragraph in the text and all lines of a block quotation five spaces.

Spacing: Double-space the entire paper, including the title page, block quotations, References, and Footnotes.

Numbering: Number your pages consecutively, starting with the title page and continuing through the list of Footnotes. The short title (the first few words or other key words of the title) should go ½ inch from the top of the page and flush with the right margin. Place the page number a double-space below the short title, flush with the right margin.

6.2.a. Title page

Title: Center on the page, capitalizing the first letter in each major word. Double-space to the first line of the heading.

Heading: An accepted form for a student paper consists of your name, the course, your instructor's name, and the date, each typed on a separate, centered line. Double-space the heading.

If you are submitting your paper for publication, center your name a double-space below the title. Center the university name a double-space below your name. If the department is not psychology, enter the department name double-spaced between your name and the university, also centered.

Running head: If you are submitting your paper for publication, type in capital letters a shortened version of the title, maximum 50 characters, centered and 1½ inches from the bottom of the page.

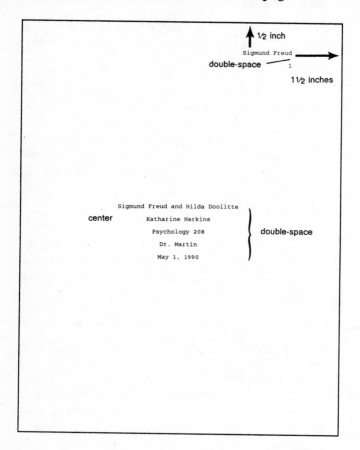

½ inch

Sigmund Freud

double-space · 1

1½ inches

center — Sigmund Freud and Hilda Doolitte
Katharine Harkins
Psychology 208
Dr. Martin
May 1, 1990

} double-space

6.2.b. Abstract

Type the abstract (a summary of the paper) on a separate page following the title page.

Title: Center *Abstract* 1½ inches from the top of the page.

First line: Begin the paragraph a double-space below the title, and do not indent the first line.

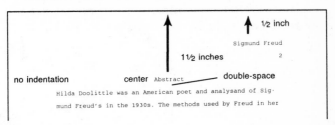

6.2.c. Text

Begin the text on a new page following the Abstract.

Title: Center the title 1½ inches from the top of the page.

First line: Begin a double-space below the title, and indent five spaces.

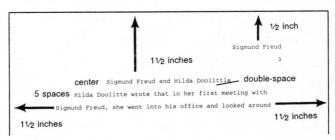

6.2.d. References

The list of References follows the text. Arrange the list alphabetically by the first author's last name or by the first word of the title (excluding *A*, *An*, or *The*), if the author is unknown.

Title: Center *References* 1½ inches from top of the first page only of your list. Double-space to the first entry.

Indentation: Begin each entry flush left and indent each subsequent line in an entry three spaces from the left margin.

Spacing: Double-space between and within all entries.

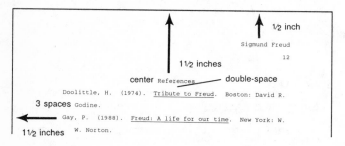

6.2.e. Footnotes

The Footnotes list follows the References.

Title: Center *Footnotes* 1½ inches from the top of the first page only of your list. Double-space to the first note.

Indentation: Indent the first line of each entry five spaces, and type all subsequent lines within the entry flush with the left margin.

Spacing: Double-space between and within all entries.

Note numbers: Number the notes consecutively, making sure each note corresponds to the correct citation in the text. Use superscript numbers.

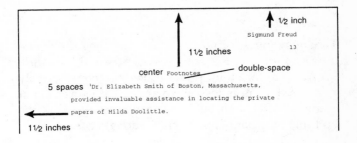

7. Note-and-Bibliography Style

7.1. Documentation

7.1.a. Notes

The following are guidelines based on the *MLA Handbook for Writers of Research Papers,* 3rd ed. (New York: MLA, 1988) for citing publications in a consecutively numbered list of notes, which appear either as a list of endnotes after your text or as footnotes typed at the bottom of the pages on which citations occur.

Books

Unlike bibliographic entries that have three main elements separated by periods, notes for books require four elements that are separated by commas: author, title, publication information (city, publisher, publication date), and page number(s). List the author's name in regular order, followed by a comma. Then list the title and any subtitle, underlining it if the source is a book, play, or long poem, or enclosing it in quotation marks if it is a short story, poem, or work in a collection. Capitalize all major words.

List the city given on the title page (or the first city if more than one are listed), and include the state or country if the city is an unfamiliar one. Shorten the publisher's name by dropping any initial article and words such as *Press, Publisher, Inc., Company* (but use *UP* for *University Press*), and by using the first or only surname if the company is named for a person or persons (*Norton* for *W. W. Norton; Farrar* for *Farrar, Straus & Giroux*). Enclose the publication information in parentheses. Do not use a comma before the publication information. Follow the publication information with a space and the page number(s) of the material cited in the text. Do not use *p.* or *pp.*

Indent the first line of each note five spaces and type subsequent lines flush with the left margin. End the note with a period.

The sample notes in this section correspond to the Works Cited entries in section 5.1.a. Consult those entries for information you need about specific elements of an entry.

— Book by one author

[1] Coates Redmon, Come as You Are: The Peace Corps Story (San Diego: Harcourt, 1986) 16-18.

— Book by two or three authors

[2] Michael Begon, John L. Harper, and Colin R. Townsend, Ecology: Individuals, Populations, and Communities (Sunderland, MA: Sinauer, 1986) 358-59.

— Book by four or more authors

Give the first name and substitute *et al.* for the other authors.

[3] Richard C. Bush, et al., The Religious World: Communities of Faith, 2nd ed. (New York: Macmillan, 1988) 101-02.

You may also use all the author's full names.

[3] Richard C. Bush, Joseph F. Byrnes, Hyla S. Converse, Kenneth Dollarhide, Azim Nanji, Robert F. Weir, and Kyle M. Yates, Jr., The Religious World: Communities of Faith, 2nd ed. (New York: Macmillan, 1988) 101-02.

— Book by a group

[4] St. Martin's Press, The St. Martin's Guide for Authors of College Textbooks (New York: St. Martin's, 1985) 39-42.

— Book with an unidentified author

[5] Hammond Compact Road Atlas and Vacation Guide (Maplewood, NJ: Hammond, 1975) 15.

— Book prepared by an editor

[6] Ellen C. Wynn, ed., The Short Story: 50 Masterpieces (New York: St. Martin's, 1983) v.

[7] Henry James, The Portrait of a Lady, ed. Leon Edel (Boston: Houghton, 1963) 44-45.

[8] Leon Edel, ed., The Portrait of a Lady, by Henry James (Boston: Houghton, 1963) 3.

— Introduction, preface, foreword, or afterword

Do not capitalize the name of the part cited.

[9] Taylor Branch, preface, Parting the Waters: America in the King Years, 1954-63, by Branch (New York: Simon, 1988) xi-xii.

— Work in an edited collection

[10] August Wilson, Fences, The Bedford Introduction to Drama, ed. Lee A. Jacobus (New York: Bedford-St. Martin's, 1989) 1043-73.

— One volume of a multivolume work

[11] Randy Roberts and James S. Olson, eds., American Experiences, vol. 2 (Glenview, IL: Scott, 1986) 101.

— Edition

[12] Don Peretz, The Middle East Today, 4th ed. (New York: Praeger, 1983) 387-88.

— Translation

[13] Emmanuel Le Roy Ladurie, Montaillou: The Promised Land of Error, trans. Barbara Bray (New York: Vintage-Random, 1979) 18-19.

[14] Barbara Bray, trans., Montaillou: The Promised Land of Error, by Emmanuel Le Roy Ladurie (New York: Vintage-Random, 1979) 18-19.

— Republished book

[15] Alice Walker, You Can't Keep a Good Woman Down (1971; San Diego: Harvest-Harcourt, 1981) 29-30.

— Book in a series

[16] Bruce S. Glassman, J. Paul Getty: Oil Billionaire, The American Dream (Englewood Cliffs, NJ: Silver, 1989) 25.

— Publisher's imprint

[17] John Hersey, <u>Blues</u> (New York: Borzoi-Knopf, 1987) 67-68.

— Item from a reference book

[18] James Callahan Morton, "The West as a Factor in American Politics," <u>Encyclopedia Americana</u>, 1955 ed.

[19] "Paleontology," <u>Random House Dictionary of the English Language</u>, 1987 ed.

— Government publication

[20] United States, Cong., Senate, Committee on Foreign Relations, <u>Hearings on Armament and Disarmament Problems</u>, 90th Cong., 1st sess. (Washington: GPO, 1967) 44.

— Pamphlet

[21] Educational Testing Service, <u>Borrowing for Education</u> (Princeton, NJ: ETS, 1989) 3.

— Unpublished dissertation

[22] Anne Cahn, "Eggheads and Warheads: Scientists and the ABM," diss., MIT, 1971, 25-26.

— Published dissertation

[23] Roderic C. Botts, Influences in the Teaching of English, 1971-1935: An Illusion of Progress, diss., Northeastern U, 1970 (Ann Arbor: UMI, 1971, 71-1799) 18.

— Published proceedings of conference

[24] Elizabeth V. Spelman, "Plato and Aristotle on Women," abstract, Proceedings and Addresses of the American Philosophical Association, vol. 63, no. 2 (Newark, DE: APA, 1989) 57.

— Book published before 1900

[25] George Eliot, Middlemarch (London, 1871-72) 345.

— Non-English book

²⁶ Franz Kafka, <u>Das Schloss</u> [<u>The</u>
<u>Castle</u>] (Frankfurt am Main: Fischer, 1982)
77-78.

Periodicals

Unlike bibliographic entries that have three main elements separated by periods, notes for periodicals require four elements separated by commas: author, title, publication information, and page number(s). List the author's name in regular order, followed by a comma. Then list the title and any subtitle of the article, followed by a comma, in quotation marks. Capitalize all major words.

The journal title, volume number, and publication date comprise the publication information. List the journal title as it appears in the periodical, omitting any initial *A*, *An*, or *The*, and capitalize all major words. Underline the title. Skip one space and give the volume number, followed by a space, the date in parentheses, a colon, a space, and the page number(s) of the material cited in the text. Do not use *p.* or *pp.*

Indent the first line of each note five spaces and type subsequent lines flush with the left margin. End the entry with a period.

The sample notes in this section correspond to the Works Cited entries in section 5.1.a. Consult those entries for information you need about specific elements of an entry.

— Article in a journal with continuous pagination

[1] Willard B. Gatewood, Jr., "Aristocrats of Color: South and North: The Black Elite, 1880-1920," Journal of Southern History 54 (1988): 19.

— Article in a journal paginated by issue

[2] Adlai E. Stevenson and Alton Frye, "Trading with the Communists," Foreign Affairs 68.2 (1989): 70.

— Article from a newspaper

[3] Sam Hemingway, "Slain British 'Spy' Trailed," Burlington Free Press 15 Apr. 1990: A1.

— Article from a magazine

[4] Adam Begley, "Black Studies' New Star," New York Times Magazine 1 Apr. 1990: 42.

— Article from a magazine, unidentified author

[5] "Gorbachev's Greatest Gamble," Economist 24-30 Mar. 1990: 17.

— Editorial or letter to the editor

Do not capitalize the labels *editorial* or *letter*.

[6] "Mitterand's East Bank," editorial,
Wall Street Journal 6 Apr. 1990, eastern
ed.: A18.

[7] David Hildebrand, letter, Pennsyl-
vania Gazette, Feb.-Mar. 1990: 17.

— Review

Do not capitalize the label *rev. of*.

[8] Marilynne Robinson, "The Guilt She
Left Behind," rev. of Because It Is Bitter,
and Because It Is My Heart, by Joyce Carol
Oates, New York Times Book Review 23 Apr
1990: 7-9.

Other sources

The following sources do not fall under the book or
periodical categories. Unlike bibliographic entries that
are divided by periods, the elements in the following
entries are separated by commas. Follow guidelines
particular to each entry.

— Computer software

Do not capitalize the labels *vers.* or *computer
software*.

[1] Steven S. Sargent, <u>The First Crusade: The Great Expedition to Jerusalem</u>, vers. 1.0, computer software, Clearinghouse for Academic Software, 1987, Digital VAX.

— **Material from a computer service**

[2] "Thomas Jefferson," <u>Academic American Encyclopedia</u>, 1981 (CompuServe record no. 1823).

— **Material from an information service**

[3] Mary F. Belenky, "The Role of Deafness in the Moral Development of Hearing Impaired Children and Adolescents," <u>Teaching, Learning and Development</u>, ed. A. Areson and J. DeCaro (Rochester, NY: National Institute for the Deaf, 1984) 115 (ERIC ED 248 646).

— **Letter**

[4] George Kennan, "Letter to his sister," 7 Dec. 1940, <u>Sketches from a Life</u> (New York: Pantheon, 1989) 47-48.

[5] Richard Leakey, letter to the author, 24 July 1985.

[6] Henry Lee Higginson, letter to his father, 29 Sept. 1989, Henry Lee Higginson Papers, Lamont Library, Cambridge, MA.

— **Interview**

Do not capitalize the label *interview*.

[7] Barbara Tuchman, interview, A World of Ideas, by Bill Moyers (New York: Doubleday, 1989) 12.

[8] Jim Lehrer, personal interview, 2 Oct. 1986.

[9] David Lynch, interview, All Things Considered, National Public Radio, WNYC, New York, 12 Apr. 1990.

— **Television or radio program**

[10] "Comfortable Lies and Bitter Truths," writ. and narr. Hedrick Smith, prod. and dir. Sherry Jones, Inside Gorbachev's USSR, exec. prod. WGBH, PBS, WNET, New York, 7 May 1990.

— Film, videotape

[11] *Driving Miss Daisy*, dir. Bruce Beresford, with Jessica Tandy, Morgan Freeman, and Dan Aykroyd, Warner, 1989.

[12] Morgan Freeman, actor, *Driving Miss Daisy*, dir. Bruce Beresford, with Jessica Tandy and Dan Aykroyd, Warner, 1989.

— Performance

[13] *Lettice and Lovage*, by Peter Shaffer, dir. Michael Blakemore, with Maggie Smith, Barrymore Theater, New York, 2 Apr. 1990.

[14] Michael Blakemore, dir., *Lettice and Lovage*, by Peter Shaffer, with Maggie Smith, Barrymore Theater, New York, 2 Apr. 1990.

— Recording

[15] Charlie Parker, alto saxophone, "Blues for Alice," rec. Aug. 1951, *The Original Recordings of Charlie Parker*, Polygram, 837176-2, 1988.

[16] Franz Joseph Haydn, Symphony no. 93 in D major and Surprise, Symphony no. 94 in G major, cond. George Szell, Cleveland Orch., Columbia, MS 7006.

— Musical composition

[17] Franz Joseph Haydn, Surprise, Symphony no. 94 in G Major.

— Work of art

[18] Georges Seurat, A Sunday Afternoon on the Island of La Grande Jatte, Art Institute of Chicago, Chicago.

— Photograph of a work of art

[19] James A. McNeill Whistler, Peacock Room from Home of F. R. Leyland, Freer Gallery of Art, Washington, DC, illus. 21-91 in Art through the Ages, 8th ed., by Horst de la Croix and Richard G. Tansey (San Diego: Harcourt, 1986).

— Lecture, speech, or address

[20] William Safire, commence. address, Syracuse Univ., Syracuse, NY, 6 May 1990.

Subsequent references to the same work

The first time you cite a work in your list of Notes, give the complete bibliographic information. For subsequent references to the same work, use a short notation.

¹ Coates Redmon, Come as You Are: The Peace Corps Story (San Diego: Harcourt, 1986) 16-18.

² Stephen Wayne and George C. Edwards, Presidential Leadership: Politics and Policy Making (New York: St. Martin's, 1985) 35-36.

³ Redmon 89.

⁴ Stephen Wayne and George C. Edwards, Studying the Presidency (New York: St. Martin's, 1983) 109.

⁵ Wayne and Edwards, Studying 211.

7.1.b. Bibliography

You may or may not need to include a Bibliography with Notes. Check with your instructor. If in doubt, include a Bibliography, following the form given for the list of Works Cited in 5.1.a. Use the heading *Bibliography* rather than *Works Cited*.

7.1.c. In-text citations

Number references consecutively throughout the paper, beginning with 1. The numbers should be superscript and should always follow punctuation, except dashes. Generally, place the note number at the end of the sentence, clause, or phrase that includes material quoted, paraphrased, summarized, or otherwise referred to.

— Text

Détente was based on mutual restraint, meaning that while the United States had to
resist Soviet interference in other areas
of the world it should also be willing to
expand relations in the context of respon-
sible behavior.[1]

— Note

Note

[1] Henry Kissinger, The White House
Years (Boston: Little, 1979) 128-30.

7.2. Sample pages

See the instructions for preparing a paper according to MLA style in section 5.2.

7.2.a. Heading and title

See the instructions for the heading and title in section 5.2.a.

7.2.b. Endnotes

Title: Center *Notes* one inch from the top of the first page only of your list. Double-space to the first note.

Margins: One inch on all sides; do not justify lines.

Indentation: Begin each note by indenting five spaces and typing the superscript note number. Skip a space to the author's name. All subsequent lines in an individual entry should be flush with the left margin.

Spacing: Double-space between and within all endnotes.

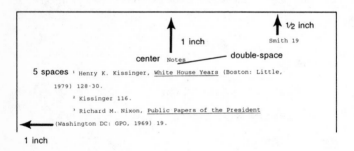

7.2.c. Bibliography

Follow instructions for preparing the list of Works Cited in section 5.2.c. Use the heading *Bibliography* instead of *Works Cited*.

7.2.d. Footnotes

If your instructor asks you to use footnotes in your text instead of endnotes, follow the guidelines below.

Placement: Begin footnotes four lines below the last line of text on the page that contains the citation. If the note continues onto the next page, continue it below a solid line typed a double-space below the last line of text on the new page. Footnotes corresponding to the new page immediately follow this continued note.

Indentation: Begin each footnote by indenting five spaces and typing the superscript note number. Skip a space to the author's name. All subsequent lines in an individual entry should be flush with the left margin.

Spacing: Single-space within footnotes; double-space between notes.

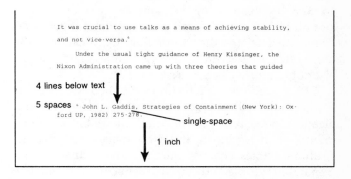

8. Council of Biology Editors (CBE) Style

8.1. Documentation

8.1.a. Literature Cited

The following are guidelines based on the *CBE Style Manual: A Guide for Authors, Editors, and Publishers in the Biological Sciences*, 5th ed., rev. and exp. (Bethesda, MD: CBE, 1983) for citing sources in your list of Literature Cited. The models that follow represent the number system. If you are using the name-and-year system, do not number the entries; ask your instructor if you need to list the date after the author. For a clarification of the two styles, see section 3.4. For guidelines on typing the list of Literature Cited, see section 8.2.

CBE Literature Cited entries for books consist of author, title, and publication information (city of publication, publisher, year of publication). Separate elements with a period and two spaces. Reverse all authors' names and use only initials for first names. Separate multiple authors with semicolons. Capitalize only the first word and any proper names or proper adjectives in book and article titles. Do not underline titles or use quotation marks.

List the city as it appears on the title page (or list only the first if more than one are listed) and the state or country if the city is an unfamiliar one. Give complete publishers' names, but abbreviate *Univ.* when used. Add a semicolon and a space after the publisher and list the date.

CBE entries for periodicals consist of author, article title, journal title, volume number (and issue number, if any), page numbers, and the date. Treat punctuation, authors' names, and article titles as you would for books. Abbreviate journal titles according to common use in the field; do not underline. List the volume number, add a colon, and give the inclusive page numbers of the article. Add a semicolon and a space and list the date.

If you are using the number system, check with your instructor whether you should list the works in the order in which they were cited in your text or list them alphabetically by author and then number them consecutively. Number each entry and indent the subsequent lines of an entry as shown in the models that follow.

If you are using the name-and-year system, arrange the Literature Cited list alphabetically by author. List two or more works by the same author chronologically. If two or more works by the same author were published in the same year, arrange the entries alphabetically within that year and assign lowercase letters (1988a, 1988b). Do not number the entries. Start each entry flush with the left margin and indent subsequent lines five spaces.

— **Book by one author**

```
1. McIntyre, J. W.  Spirit of northern
      lakes.  Minneapolis, MN: Univ. of Min-
      nesota Press; 1988.
```

— **Book by two or more authors**

```
2. Mark, V. H.; Ervin, F. R.  Violence and
      the brain.  New York: Harper & Row;
      1970.
```

— Publication by a group

3. Committee on Arctic Social Science.
   Arctic social agenda: an agenda for ac-
   tion. Washington, DC: National Academy
   Press; 1989.

— Book prepared by an editor

4. Huxley, J., editor. The new sys-
   tematics. New York: Clarendon Press;
   1940.

— Work in an edited collection

5. Ford, E. B. Polymorphism and taxonomy.
   In: Juxley, J., ed. The new sys-
   tematics. New York: Clarendon Press;
   1940:493-513.

— Multivolume work

6. Roth, J.; Ruzek, S., editors. Research
   in the sociology of care. Greenwich,
   CT: JAI Press; 1985. 4 vol.

— One volume of a multivolume work

7. Roth, J.; Ruzek, S., editors. Research in the sociology of care. Vol. 4. Greenwich, CT: JAI Press; 1985.

— Article in a journal with continuous pagination

8. Krause, D. W. Paleocene primates from western Canada. Canadian J. Earth Sciences. 15:1250-1271; 1987.

— Article in a journal paginated by issue

9. Strong, P. I. V.; Bissonette, J. A. Feeding and chick-rearing areas of Common Loons. J. Wild. Manage. 53(1):72-76; 1989.

— Article from a newspaper

10. Fields, G. Occupational health becomes a specialty for more physicians. The Wall Street Journal. 1978 Oct. 24:18 (col. 1).

— Government publication

11. U.S. Congress, Senate. Arctic research
    and policy act. Public law 98-373. 98
    Stat. 1248. Ninety-eighth Congress,
    second session. 1984 July 31. Avail-
    able from: U.S. Government Printing Of-
    fice. Washington, DC.

— Unpublished dissertation

12. Fernando, M. H. J. P. Predation of the
    glasshouse red spider mite by
    Phytoseiulus persimilis. London: Univ.
    of London; 1977. Dissertation.

— Published proceedings of conference

13. McIntyre, J. W. Status of Common Loons
    in New York from a historical perspec-
    tive. Sutcliffe, S., ed. Proc. N.
    Amer. Conf. Common Loon Res. Manage.
    2:117-122; 1979.

14. Purser, J. M. <u>Greenhaus</u>. Vers. 1.0
    [Computer software]. Ames, IA: The
    Clearinghouse for Academic Software,
    1987. Digital VAX.

8.1.b. Parenthetical citations

A parenthetical citation follows any quotation, paraphrase, summary, or reference to another's work. Your goal is to give the author credit and the reader enough information to find the complete reference in the Literature Cited and to locate the exact material in the cited source.

Number system

If you are using the number system, your in-text citations will be the numbers that correspond to the Literature Cited entries. Use the same number assigned to a source each time you refer to that source.

— Author mentioned in text

McIntyre (13) divides vocal communication
into four categories.

— No author mentioned

There is a significant correlation between intensity of disturbance and number of breeding loon pair (7).

— More than one source in citation

Loons have been able to recover from past dips in their population (5, 1).

Name-and-year system

If you are using the name-and-year system, your citations will include the author (or a short form of the title if no author is given) and the year of publication. Two ways of incorporating citations are shown in the first two examples that follow. The first shows the author and publication year in parentheses at the end of the sentence. Use the second method if you wish to bring more attention to the author by using his or her name in the text. You then need only put the year in parentheses immediately following the author's name.

— Author named in citation

Vocal communication is divided into four categories (McIntyre 1988).

— Author named in text

McIntyre (1988) divides vocal communication into four categories.

— A work by two authors

Strong and Bissonette (1989) offer management techniques designed to preserve the feeding grounds.

— Three or more authors

Heimberger et al. (1983) found on lakes in central Ontario that dense development around loon nests reduced reproductive success.

— Corporate author

The assertions made by the Committee on Arctic Social Sciences (1989) correspond with the research done by the Polar Research Board.

— Author of more than one reference in the same year

On lakes in northern Alberta, Vermeer
(1973a) did find a significant correlation
between intensity of disturbance and number
of breeding loon pair.

— More than one source in citation

List the works in chronological order and separate them
with commas.

Loons have been able to recover from past
dips in their population (Titus and Van
Druff 1981, McIntyre 1989).

— Indirect source for a reference

Include entries for both the direct and the indirect
sources in the Literature Cited list.

In New Hampshire a 53 percent decline in
the loon population was reported in 1978
(Sutcliffe 1978, cited by McIntyre 1988).

8.1.c. Footnotes

Use footnotes only to give further explanatory or bibliographic information that is important to your text but
would not fit smoothly in the running text.

Number notes consecutively in the text with superscript numbers. List entries consecutively in the list of

Footnotes, again with superscript numbers, indenting the first line of each footnote five spaces. Footnotes are typed on a separate page directly after the Literature Cited list.

— Text

Before 1975, loons had not been seen breeding for a century in Massachusetts. But by 1984 there were six breeding pairs on Quabbin Reservoir.[1]

— Note

Footnotes

[1]When a town in central Massachusetts was flooded to create Quabbin Reservoir, none of the toxic metals were properly removed beforehand. This may have contributed to the acidification of the water.

8.2. Sample pages

The following guidelines for preparing your paper are based on CBE recommendations. Because CBE style is used predominantly in journals, some of its instructions have been adapted to the requirements of student papers.

Your paper should include the following elements. Begin each on a new page.

a) Title, author, course, and date (and your address if the paper is being submitted for publication)
b) Abstract (a summary of the paper)
c) Text
d) Acknowledgments (acknowledging people or groups instrumental in your research)
e) Literature Cited
f) Footnotes
g) Legend for figures (if not included on the pages where the figures appear)

Margins: Allow between 1 and 1½ inches on all sides. Do not divide a word at the end of a line.

Indentation: Indent the first line of each text paragraph and all lines of any quotations longer than four typed lines five spaces.

Spacing: Double-space the entire manuscript, including the Literature Cited and Footnotes lists.

Numbering: Number pages consecutively, beginning with the title page. Type the number in the upper right-hand corner, flush with the right margin. Include a short version of the title one space before the number.

8.2.a. Title page

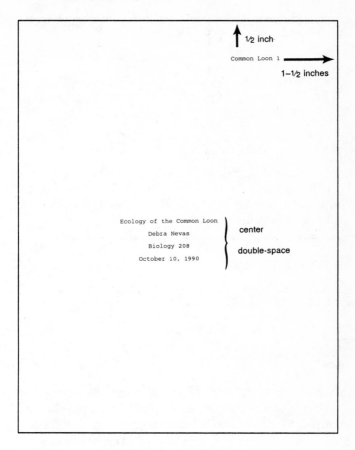

8.2.b. Text

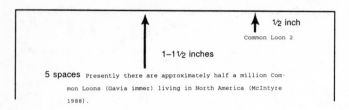

1–1½ inches

5 spaces Presently there are approximately half a million Common Loons (Gavia immer) living in North America (McIntyre 1988).

8.2.c. Literature Cited

If you are using the number system, arrange the entries in the order in which they are cited in the text, or alphabetically by author and number consecutively. Check with your instructor.

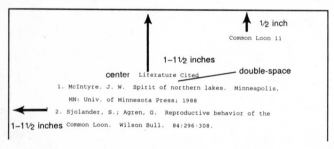

½ inch

Common Loon 11

1–1½ inches

center Literature Cited   double-space

1. McIntyre. J. W. Spirit of northern lakes. Minneapolis, MN: Univ. of Minnesota Press; 1988

2. Sjolander, S.; Agren, G. Reproductive behavior of the Common Loon. Wilson Bull. 84:296-308.

1–1½ inches

If you are using the name-and-year system, list the entries alphabetically by author and do not number the entries. Start the first line of an entry flush with the left margin. Indent subsequent lines of an entry five spaces.

Index

Documentation samples are identified by style: APA (American Psychological Association), CBE (Council of Biology Editors), MLA (Modern Language Association), and N-and-B (note-and-bibliography).